Firearm Violence, 1993-2011

Michael Planty, Ph.D., and Jennifer L. Truman, Ph.D., *BJS Statisticians*

In 2011, a total of 478,400 fatal and nonfatal violent crimes were committed with a firearm (table 1). Homicides made up about 2% of all firearm-related crimes. There were 11,101 firearm homicides in 2011, down by 39% from a high of 18,253 in 1993 (figure 1). The majority of the decline in firearm-related homicides occurred between 1993 and 1998. Since 1999, the number of firearm homicides increased from 10,828 to 12,791 in 2006 before declining to 11,101 in 2011.

Nonfatal firearm-related violent victimizations against persons age 12 or older declined 70%, from 1.5 million in 1993 to 456,500 in 2004 (figure 2). The number then fluctuated between about 400,000 to 600,000 through 2011.[1] While the number of firearm crimes declined over time, the percentage of all violence that involved a firearm did not change substantively, fluctuating between 6% and 9% over the same period. In 1993, 9% of all violence was committed with a firearm, compared to 8% in 2011.

[1]Many percentages and counts presented in this report are based on nonfatal firearm victimizations. Since firearm homicides accounted for about 2% of all firearm victimizations, when firearm homicides are included in the total firearm estimates, the findings do not change significantly.

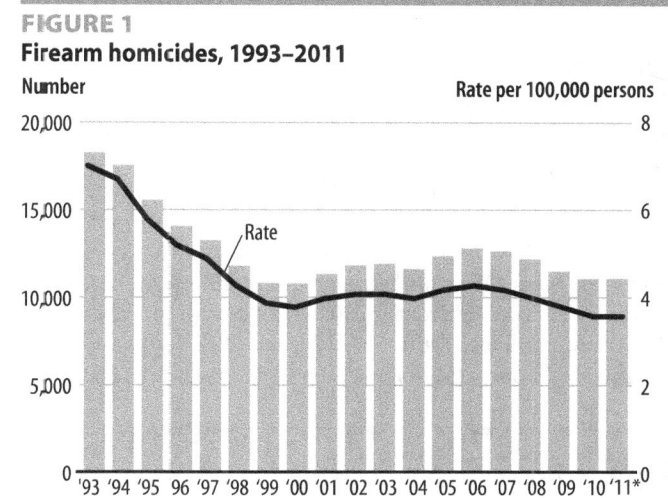

FIGURE 1

Firearm homicides, 1993–2011

Note: Excludes homicides due to legal intervention and operations of war. See appendix table 1 for numbers and rates.

*Preliminary estimates retrieved from Hoyert DL, Xu JQ. (2012) Deaths: Preliminary data for 2011. *National Vital Statistics Reports*, 61(6).

Source: Centers for Disease Control and Prevention, National Center for Injury Prevention and Control. Web-based Injury Statistics Query and Reporting System (WISQARS), 1993–2010. Retrieved March 2013 from www.cdc.gov/ncipc/wisqars.

HIGHLIGHTS

- Firearm-related homicides declined 39%, from 18,253 in 1993 to 11,101 in 2011.

- Nonfatal firearm crimes declined 69%, from 1.5 million victimizations in 1993 to 467,300 victimizations in 2011.

- For both fatal and nonfatal firearm victimizations, the majority of the decline occurred during the 10-year period from 1993 to 2002.

- Firearm violence accounted for about 70% of all homicides and less than 10% of all nonfatal violent crime from 1993 to 2011.

- About 70% to 80% of firearm homicides and 90% of nonfatal firearm victimizations were committed with a handgun from 1993 to 2011.

- From 1993 to 2010, males, blacks, and persons ages 18 to 24 had the highest rates of firearm homicide.

- In 2007-11, about 23% of victims of nonfatal firearm crime were injured.

- About 61% of nonfatal firearm violence was reported to the police in 2007-11.

- In 2007-11, less than 1% of victims in all nonfatal violent crimes reported using a firearm to defend themselves during the incident.

- In 2004, among state prison inmates who possessed a gun at the time of offense, less than 2% bought their firearm at a flea market or gun show and 40% obtained their firearm from an illegal source.

The primary source of information on firearm-related homicides was obtained from mortality data based on death certificates in the National Vital Statistics System of the National Center for Health Statistics (NCHS), Centers for Disease Control and Prevention's (CDC) Web-based Injury Statistics Query and Reporting System (WISQARS). These mortality data include causes of death reported by attending physicians, medical examiners, and coroners, and demographic information about decedents reported by funeral directors who obtain that information from family members and other informants. The NCHS collects, compiles, verifies, and prepares these data for release to the public.

The estimates of nonfatal violent victimization are based on data from the Bureau of Justice Statistics' (BJS) National Crime Victimization Survey (NCVS), which collects information on nonfatal crimes against persons age 12 or older reported and not reported to the police from a nationally representative sample of U.S. households. Homicide rates are presented per 100,000 persons and the nonfatal victimization rates are presented per 1,000 persons age 12 or older. Additional information on firearm violence in this report comes from the School-Associated Violent Deaths Surveillance Study (SAVD), the FBI's Supplemental Homicide Reports (SHR), the Survey of Inmates in State

Correctional Facilities (SISCF), and the Survey of Inmates in Federal Correctional Facilities (SIFCF). Each source provides different information about victims and incident characteristics. Estimates are shown for different years based on data availability and measures of reliability. (For more information about these sources, see *Methodology*.)

FIGURE 2
Nonfatal firearm victimizations, 1993–2011

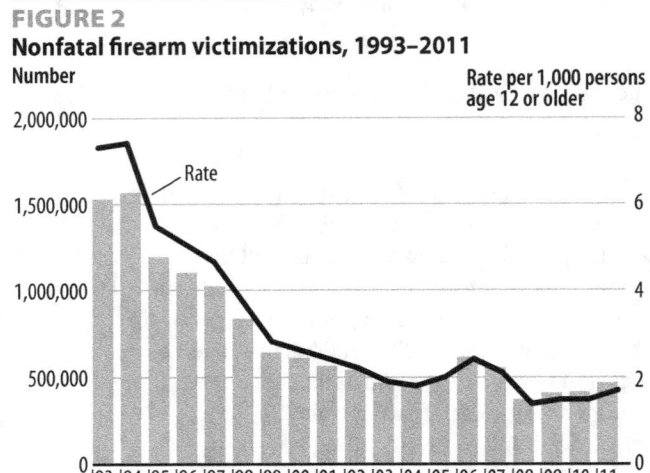

Note: See appendix table 2 for numbers, rates, and standard errors.
Source: Bureau of Justice Statistics, National Crime Victimization Survey, 1993–2011.

TABLE 1
Criminal firearm violence, 1993–2011

Year	Total fatal and nonfatal firearm violence	Firearm homicides	Nonfatal firearm victimizations[a]	Nonfatal firearm incidents[b]	Rate of nonfatal firearm victimization[c]	All violence involving firearms	All firearm violence that was homicide
			Number			Percent	
1993	1,548,000	18,253	1,529,700	1,222,700	7.3	9.2%	1.2%
1994	1,585,700	17,527	1,568,200	1,287,200	7.4	9.3	1.1
1995	1,208,800	15,551	1,193,200	1,028,900	5.5	7.9	1.3
1996	1,114,800	14,037	1,100,800	939,500	5.1	7.9	1.3
1997	1,037,300	13,252	1,024,100	882,900	4.7	7.7	1.3
1998	847,200	11,798	835,400	673,300	3.8	7.0	1.4
1999	651,700	10,828	640,900	523,600	2.9	6.1	1.7
2000	621,000	10,801	610,200	483,700	2.7	7.3	1.7
2001	574,500	11,348	563,100	507,000	2.5	7.7	2.0
2002	551,800	11,829	540,000	450,800	2.3	7.4	2.1
2003	479,300	11,920	467,300	385,000	2.0	6.2	2.5
2004	468,100	11,624	456,500	405,800	1.9	6.9	2.5
2005	515,900	12,352	503,500	446,400	2.1	7.4	2.4
2006	627,200	12,791	614,400	552,000	2.5	7.4	2.0
2007	567,400	12,632	554,800	448,400	2.2	8.3	2.2
2008	383,500	12,179	371,300	331,600	1.5	6.0	3.2
2009	421,600	11,493	410,100	383,400	1.6	7.4	2.7
2010	426,100	11,078	415,000	378,800	1.6	8.6	2.6
2011[d]	478,400	11,101	467,300	414,600	1.8	8.2	2.3

Note: See appendix table 3 for standard errors.
[a]A victimization refers to a single victim that experienced a criminal incident.
[b]An incident is a specific criminal act involving one or more victims or victimizations.
[c]Per 1,000 persons age 12 or older.
[d]Preliminary homicide estimates retrieved from Hoyert DL, Xu JQ. (2012) Deaths: Preliminary data for 2011. *National Vital Statistics Reports,* 61(6).
Sources: Bureau of Justice Statistics, National Crime Victimization Survey, 1993–2011; and Centers for Disease Control and Prevention, National Center for Injury Prevention and Control, Web-based Injury Statistics Query and Reporting System (WISQARS), 1993–2010. Retrieved March 2013 from www.cdc.gov/ncipc/wisqars.

Trend estimates of nonfatal firearm violence are presented as annual 1-year averages or 2-year rolling averages, as noted in each table or figure. For ease of presentation, 2-year estimates are referenced according to the most recent year. For example, estimates reported for 2011 represent the average estimates for 2010 and 2011. Other tables in this report focus on a single 5-year aggregate period from 2007 through 2011. These approaches—using rolling averages and aggregating years—increase the reliability and stability of estimates, which facilitiates comparisons over time and between subgroups.

The majority of firearm crimes were committed with a handgun

From 1993 to 2011, about 60% to 70% of homicides were committed with a firearm (table 2). Over the same period, between 6% and 9% of all nonfatal violent victimizations were committed with a firearm, with about 20% to 30% of robberies and 22% to 32% of aggravated assaults involving a firearm.

Handguns accounted for the majority of both homicide and nonfatal firearm violence (table 3). A handgun was used in about 83% of all firearm homicides in 1994, compared to 73% in 2011. Other types of firearms, such as shotguns and rifles, accounted for the remainder of firearm homicides. For nonfatal firearm violence, about 9 in 10 were committed with a handgun, and this remained stable from 1994 to 2011.

TABLE 2

Percent of violence involving a firearm, by type of crime, 1993–2011

Year	Homicide	Nonfatal violence[a]	Robbery	Aggravated assault
1993	71.2%	9.1%	22.3%	30.7%
1994	71.4	9.2	27.1	31.9
1995	69.0	7.8	27.3	28.0
1996	68.0	7.8	24.6	25.7
1997	68.0	7.6	19.9	27.0
1998	65.9	7.0	20.1	26.5
1999	64.1	6.0	19.2	22.4
2000	64.4	7.2	21.1	26.6
2001[b]	55.9	7.5	29.5	26.0
2002	67.1	7.3	23.4	28.7
2003	67.2	6.1	22.4	22.2
2004	67.0	6.8	19.7	23.6
2005	68.2	7.2	21.8	25.7
2006	68.9	7.3	16.6	24.3
2007	68.8	8.1	20.0	32.6
2008	68.3	5.8	19.6	24.6
2009	68.4	7.2	27.0	23.2
2010	68.1	8.4	24.7	25.4
2011[c]	69.6	8.0	25.7	30.6

Note: See appendix table 4 for standard errors.

[a]Nonfatal violence includes rape, sexual assault, robbery, aggravated and simple assault. A small percentage of rape and sexual assaults involved firearms but are not shown in table due to small sample sizes.

[b]The homicide estimates that occurred as a result of the events of September 11, 2001, are included in the total number of homicides.

[c]Preliminary homicide estimates retrieved from Hoyert DL, Xu JQ. (2012) Deaths: Preliminary data for 2011. National Vital Statistics Reports, 61(6).

Sources: Bureau of Justice Statistics, National Crime Victimization Survey, 1993–2011; and Centers for Disease Control and Prevention, National Center for Injury Prevention and Control, Web-based Injury Statistics Query and Reporting System (WISQARS), 1993–2010. Retrieved March 2013 from www.cdc.gov/ncipc/wisqars.

TABLE 3

Criminal firearm violence, by type of firearm, 1994–2011

	Homicide				Nonfatal violence					
	Handgun		Other firearm*		Handgun		Other firearm*		Gun type unknown	
Year	Annual number	Percent	Annual number	Percent	Average annual number	Percent	Average annual number	Percent	Average annual number	Percent
1994	13,510	82.7%	2,830	17.3%	1,387,100	89.5%	150,200	9.7%	11,700!	0.8%!
1995	12,090	81.9	2,670	18.1	1,240,200	89.8	132,800	9.6	7,700!	0.6!
1996	10,800	81.1	2,510	18.9	999,600	87.1	141,000	12.3	6,400!	0.6!
1997	9,750	78.8	2,630	21.2	894,200	84.2	159,800	15.0	8,400!	0.8!
1998	8,870	80.4	2,160	19.6	783,400	84.3	141,100	15.2	5,300!	0.6!
1999	8,010	78.8	2,150	21.2	659,600	89.4	74,100	10.0	4,500!	0.6!
2000	8,020	78.6	2,190	21.4	555,800	88.8	65,300	10.4	4,500!	0.7!
2001	7,820	77.9	2,220	22.1	506,600	86.3	65,900	11.2	14,100!	2.4!
2002	8,230	75.8	2,620	24.2	471,600	85.5	63,200	11.5	16,700!	3.0!
2003	8,890	80.3	2,180	19.7	436,100	86.6	53,200	10.6	14,400!	2.9!
2004	8,330	78.0	2,350	22.0	391,700	84.8	53,400	11.6	16,900!	3.7!
2005	8,550	75.1	2,840	24.9	410,600	85.5	56,200	11.7	13,200!	2.8!
2006	9,060	77.0	2,700	23.0	497,400	89.0	47,600	8.5	14,000!	2.5!
2007	8,570	73.6	3,080	26.4	509,700	87.2	65,600	11.2	9,300!	1.6!
2008	7,930	71.8	3,120	28.2	400,700	86.5	57,400	12.4	5,000!	1.1!
2009	7,370	71.3	2,970	28.7	348,700	89.2	37,600	9.6	4,400!	1.1!
2010	6,920	69.6	3,030	30.4	382,100	92.6	26,700	6.5	3,800!	0.9!
2011	7,230	72.9	2,690	27.1	389,400	88.3	49,700	11.3	2,100!	0.5!

Note: Nonfatal violence data based on 2-year rolling averages beginning in 1993. Homicide data are presented as annual estimates. See appendix table 5 for standard errors.

*Includes rifle, shotgun, and other types of firearms.

! Interpret with caution. Estimate based on 10 or fewer sample cases, or coefficient of variation is greater than 50%.

Sources: Bureau of Justice Statistics, National Crime Victimization Survey, 1993–2011; and FBI, Supplementary Homicide Reports, 1994–2011.

Males, blacks, and persons ages 18 to 24 were most likely to be victims of firearm violence

Sex

In 2010, the rate of firearm homicide for males was 6.2 per 100,000, compared to 1.1 for females (figure 3). Firearm homicide for males declined by 49% (from 12.0 per 100,000 males in 1993 to 6.2 in 2010), compared to a 51% decline for females (from 2.3 per 100,000 females in 1993 to 1.1 in 2010). The majority of the decline for both males and females occurred in the first part of the period (1993 to 2000). Over the more recent 10-year period from 2001 to 2010, the decline in firearm homicide for both males and females slowed, resulting in about a 10% decline each.

FIGURE 3
Firearm homicides, by sex, 1993–2010

Rate per 100,000 persons

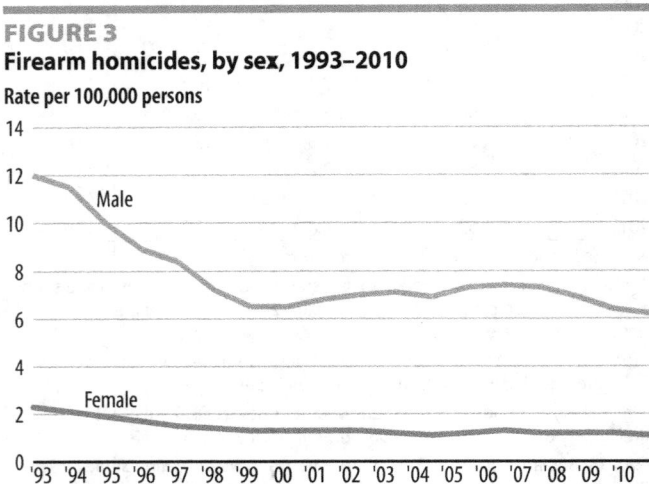

Note: See appendix table 6 for numbers and rates.

Source: Centers for Disease Control and Prevention, National Center for Injury Prevention and Control, Web-based Injury Statistics Query and Reporting System (WISQARS), 1993–2010. Retrieved March 2013 from www.cdc.gov/ncipc/wisqars.

In 2011, the rate of nonfatal firearm violence for males (1.9 per 1,000 males) was not significantly different than the rate for females (1.6 per 1,000) (figure 4). From 1994 to 2011, the rate of nonfatal firearm violence for males declined 81%, from 10.1 to 1.9 per 1,000 males. During the same period, the rate of nonfatal firearm violence against females dropped 67%, from 4.7 to 1.6 per 1,000 females. As with fatal firearm violence, the majority of the decline occurred in the first part of the period. From 2002 to 2011, the rate of nonfatal firearm violence for males declined 35%, while there was no no statistical change in the rate for females.

FIGURE 4
Nonfatal firearm violence, by sex, 1994–2011

Rate per 1,000 persons age 12 or older

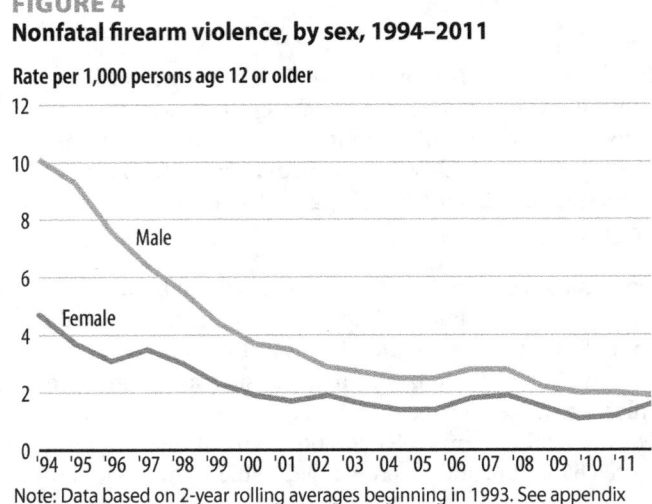

Note: Data based on 2-year rolling averages beginning in 1993. See appendix table 7 for rates and standard errors.

Source: Bureau of Justice Statistics, National Crime Victimization Survey, 1993–2011.

In 2010, the rate of firearm homicide for blacks was 14.6 per 100,000, compared to 1.9 for whites, 2.7 for American Indians and Alaska Natives, and 1.0 for Asians and Pacific Islanders (figure 5). From 1993 to 2010, the rate of firearm homicides for blacks declined by 51%, down from 30.1 per 100,000 blacks, compared to a 48% decline for whites and a 43% decline for American Indians and Alaska Natives. Asian and Pacific Islanders declined 79% over the same period, from 4.6 to 1.0 per 100,000. Although blacks experienced a decline similar to whites and American Indians and Alaska Natives, the rate of firearm homicide for blacks was 5 to 6 times higher than every other racial group in 2010. As with other demographic groups, the majority of the decline occurred in the first part of the period and slowed from 2001 to 2010.

The rate of firearm homicide for both Hispanics and non-Hispanics was about 4 per 100,000 each in 2010 (figure 6). However, the Hispanic rate had a larger and more consistent decline over time. The Hispanic rate declined 54% from 1993 to 2001 and declined 34% since 2001. In comparison, the non-Hispanic rate declined more slowly, down 42% from 1993 to 2001 and down 5% since 2001.

In 2011, non-Hispanic blacks (2.8 per 1,000) and Hispanics (2.2 per 1,000) had higher rates of nonfatal firearm violence than non-Hispanic whites (1.4 per 1,000) (figure 7). The rate of nonfatal firearm violence for Hispanics was not statistically different from the rate for blacks. From 1994 to 2011, the rates of nonfatal firearm violence for blacks and Hispanics both declined by 83%, compared to 74% for whites.

FIGURE 6
Firearm homicides, by Hispanic origin, 1993–2010

Rate per 100,000 persons

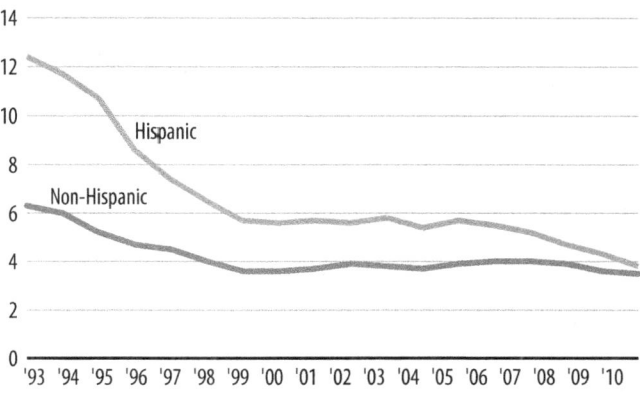

Note: See appendix table 9 for numbers and rates.

Source: Bureau of Justice Statistics, Centers for Disease Control and Prevention, National Center for Injury Prevention and Control, Web-based Injury Statistics Query and Reporting System (WISQARS), 1993–2010. Retrieved March 2013 from www.cdc.gov/ncipc/wisqars.

FIGURE 5
Firearm homicides, by race, 1993–2010

Rate per 100,000 persons

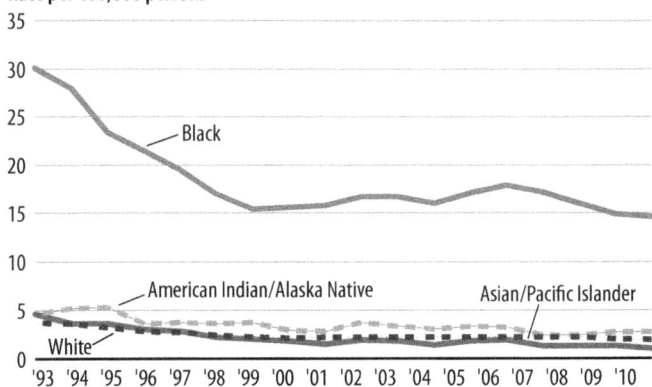

Note: See appendix table 8 for numbers and rates.

Source: Centers for Disease Control and Prevention, National Center for Injury Prevention and Control, Web-based Injury Statistics Query and Reporting System (WISQARS), 1993–2010. Retrieved March 2013 from www.cdc.gov/ncipc/wisqars.

FIGURE 7
Nonfatal firearm violence, by race and Hispanic origin, 1994–2011

Rate per 1,000 persons age 12 or older

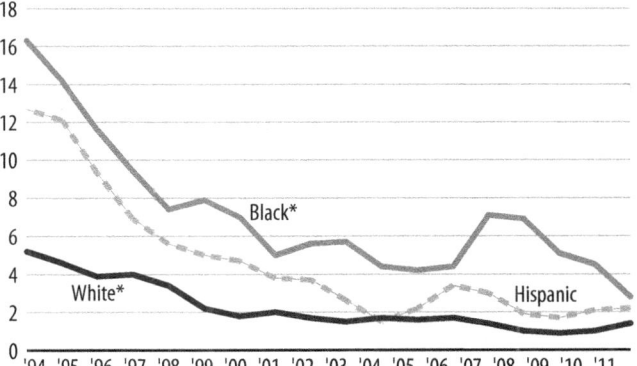

Note: Data based on 2-year rolling averages beginning in 1993. See appendix table 10 for rates and standard errors.

*Excludes persons of Hispanic or Latino origin.

Source: Bureau of Justice Statistics, National Crime Victimization Survey, 1993–2011.

Age

In 2010, the rate of firearm homicide was 10.7 per 100,000 for persons ages 18 to 24, compared to 8.1 for persons ages 25 to 34 and 0.3 for persons age 11 or younger (table 4). Firearm homicide against persons ages 18 to 34 accounted for about 30% of all firearm homicides in 2010. From 1993 to 2010, the rate of homicides for persons ages 18 to 24 declined 51%, compared to a 35% decline for persons ages 25 to 34 and 50% for persons age 11 or younger.

In 2011, persons ages 18 to 24 had the highest rate of nonfatal firearm violence (5.2 per 1,000). From 1994 to 2011, the rates of nonfatal firearm violence declined for persons ages 18 to 49, with each group declining between 72% and 77%. The rate for persons ages 12 to 17 declined 88%, from 11.4 to 1.4 per 1,000.

Persons living in urban areas had the highest rates of nonfatal firearm violence

Region

In 2010, the South had the highest rate of firearm homicides at 4.4 per 100,000 persons, compared to 3.4 in the Midwest, 3.0 in the West, and 2.8 in the Northeast (figure 8).

From 1993 to 2010, the rate of firearm homicides in the South declined by 49%, compared to a 50% decline in the Northeast, a 37% decline in the Midwest, and a 59% decline in the West.

FIGURE 8

Firearm homicides, by region, 1993–2011

Rate per 100,000 persons

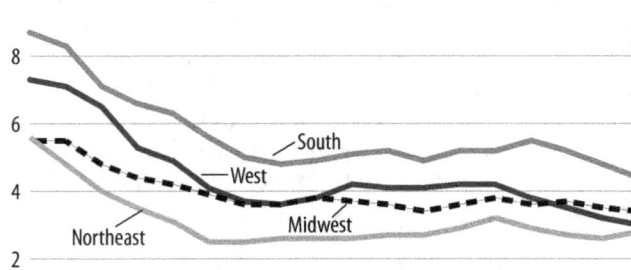

Note: See appendix table 13 for numbers and rates.

Source: Centers for Disease Control and Prevention, National Center for Injury Prevention and Control. Web-based Injury Statistics Query and Reporting System (WISQARS), 1993–2010. Retrieved March 2013 from www.cdc.gov/ncipc/wisqars).

TABLE 4

Fatal and nonfatal firearm violence, by age, 1993–2011

Year	Firearm homicide rate per 100,000 persons						Nonfatal firearm violence rate per 1,000 persons age 12 or older				
	11 or younger	12–17	18–24	25–34	35–49	50 or older	12–17	18–24	25–34	35–49	50 or older
1993	0.5	8.0	21.9	12.4	6.7	2.2	~	~	~	~	~
1994	0.4	7.8	21.2	12.0	6.3	2.1	11.4	18.1	8.7	6.3	1.6
1995	0.4	7.0	18.6	10.6	5.3	2.0	9.8	16.1	7.7	5.5	1.6
1996	0.4	5.6	17.2	9.4	4.9	1.8	7.6	12.3	6.8	4.8	1.4
1997	0.4	4.8	16.3	9.0	4.6	1.6	7.1	12.8	5.4	4.5	1.2
1998	0.3	3.7	14.4	7.9	4.2	1.5	5.7	12.4	4.5	3.8	1.0
1999	0.3	3.6	12.4	7.6	3.7	1.4	4.7	8.9	4.6	2.6	0.7
2000	0.2	2.9	12.4	7.7	3.8	1.4	3.2	7.0	3.6	2.5	1.0
2001	0.3	2.8	12.9	8.4	3.9	1.3	2.2	6.8	3.1	2.4	1.0
2002	0.3	2.9	13.0	8.8	4.0	1.4	2.4	7.3	3.1	1.8	0.8
2003	0.3	2.7	13.3	9.0	4.0	1.3	2.8	6.3	2.7	1.6	0.7
2004	0.2	3.0	11.9	8.9	3.9	1.4	1.9	3.9	2.5	2.1	0.8
2005	0.2	3.1	12.9	9.6	4.1	1.3	1.2	4.4	3.1	1.8	1.0
2006	0.3	3.6	13.6	9.6	4.1	1.4	2.3	5.6	3.4	1.8	1.0
2007	0.3	3.5	13.1	9.5	4.2	1.3	4.3	4.6	3.0	2.2	0.9
2008	0.3	3.3	12.1	9.0	4.1	1.3	3.5	3.2	2.7	1.6	0.7
2009	0.3	2.9	11.1	8.1	3.9	1.4	0.9	3.9	2.3	1.5	0.6
2010	0.3	2.8	10.7	8.1	3.6	1.4	0.6 !	5.8	2.0	1.3	0.6
2011	...	...	...	...	...	...	1.4	5.2	2.2	1.4	0.7

Note: Nonfatal firearm violence data based on 2-year rolling averages beginning in 1993. Homicide data are annual estimates. See appendix table 11 for firearm homicide numbers and appendix table 12 for nonfatal firearm violence standard errors..

~Not applicable.

...Not available.

! Interpret with caution. Estimate based on 10 or fewer sample cases, or coefficient of variation is greater than 50%.

Source: Bureau of Justice Statistics, National Crime Victimization Survey, 1993–2011; and Centers for Disease Control and Prevention, National Center for Injury Prevention and Control. Web-based Injury Statistics Query and Reporting System (WISQARS), 1993–2010. Retrieved March 2013 from www.cdc.gov/ncipc/wisqars.

In 2011, residents in the South (1.9 per 1,000) had higher rates of nonfatal firearm violence than those in the Northeast (1.3 per 1,000) (figure 9). Residents in the South (1.9 per 1,000), Midwest (1.7 per 1,000), and West (1.8 per 1,000) had statistically similar rates of nonfatal firearm violence.

Urban-rural location

The publicly available National Vital Statistics System fatal data files do not contain information about the incident's urban-rural location or population size. This information is limited to nonfatal firearm victimizations. Urban residents generally experienced the highest rate of nonfatal firearm violence (figure 10). In 2011, the rate of nonfatal firearm violence for residents in urban areas was 2.5 per 1,000, compared to 1.4 per 1,000 for suburban residents and 1.2 for rural residents. From 1994 to 2011, the rates of nonfatal firearm violence for all three locations declined between 76% and 78%.

Population size

In 2011, higher rates of nonfatal violence occurred in areas with a population of more than 250,000 residents than in areas with a population under 250,000 (table 5). From 1997 to 2011, the rates of nonfatal firearm violence for populations between 250,000 and 499,999 and 1 million residents or more declined between 57% and 62%, compared to a 37% decline for residents living in populations between 500,000 and 999,999 residents.

FIGURE 9

Nonfatal firearm violence, by region, 1997–2011

Rate per 1,000 persons age 12 or older

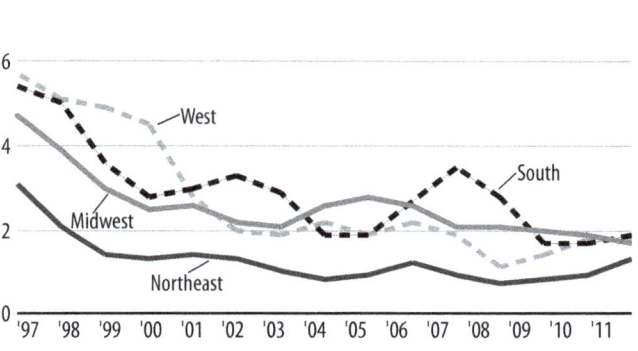

Note: Data based on 2-year rolling averages beginning in 1996. Region information was not available from 1993 to 1995. See appendix table 14 for rates and standard errors.

Source: Bureau of Justice Statistics, National Crime Victimization Survey, 1996–2011.

FIGURE 10

Nonfatal firearm violence, by urban-rural location, 1994–2011

Rate per 1,000 persons age 12 or older

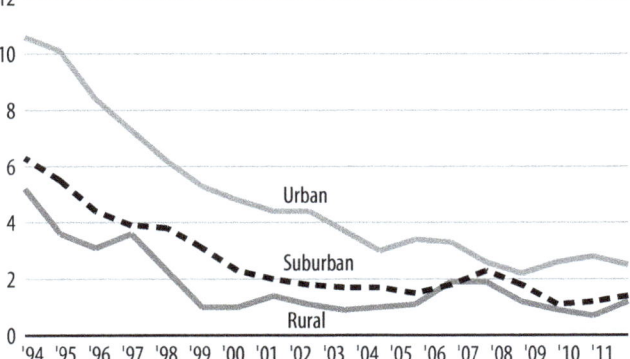

Note: Data based on 2-year rolling averages beginning in 1993. See appendix table 15 for rates and standard errors.

Source: Bureau of Justice Statistics, National Crime Victimization Survey, 1993–2011.

TABLE 5

Nonfatal firearm violence, by population size, 1997–2011

Year	Rate per 1,000 persons age 12 or older					
	Not a place*	Less than 100,000	100,000–249,999	250,000–499,999	500,000–999,999	1 million or more
1997	3.9	3.8	7.0	10.3	7.3	7.3
1998	3.0	3.9	4.8	7.0	9.2	5.7
1999	1.9	3.1	3.1	5.5	9.0	6.4
2000	1.5	2.2	3.9	6.5	6.3	5.6
2001	1.4	2.1	4.1	6.1	5.5	5.1
2002	1.2	2.3	2.8	3.9	4.9	5.3
2003	1.4	2.0	2.8	3.3	5.1	3.6
2004	1.4	1.4	3.0	4.1	5.5	2.7
2005	1.2	1.6	2.9	3.6	4.5	4.6
2006	1.6	2.1	2.6	2.6	3.8	4.9
2007	1.5	2.6	2.7	2.4	5.4	2.1
2008	0.8	2.1	2.1	3.2	4.9	1.4
2009	0.9	1.1	2.2	3.0	4.0	3.5
2010	0.9	1.2	1.8	2.8	5.1	4.0
2011	1.4	1.2	1.3	3.9	4.6	3.2

Note: Data based on 2-year rolling averages beginning in 1996. Population size information was not available from 1993 to 1995. See appendix table 16 for rates and standard errors.

*A concentration of population that is not either legally bounded as an incorporated place having an active government or delineated for statistical purposes as a census designated place with definite geographic boundaries, such as a city, town, or village.

Source: Bureau of Justice Statistics, National Crime Victimization Survey, 1996–2011.

About 11% of nonfatal violence committed by a stranger involved a firearm

Intimate partners suffered about 4.7 million nonfatal violent victimizations in the 5-year period from 2007 through 2011, and the offender used a firearm in about 4% of these victimizations (about 195,700 incidents) (table 6). Similar to intimate partner violent victimizations, offenders who were either a relative or known to the victim (e.g., a friend or acquaintance) used a firearm in about 4% to 7% of these total victimizations. In comparison, persons victimized by strangers experienced about 11 million violent victimizations, and the offender used a firearm in 11% of these victimizations.[2]

In 2007-11, the majority of nonfatal firearm violence occurred in or around the victim's home (42%) or in an open area, on the street, or while on public transportation (23%) (table 7). Less than 1% of all nonfatal firearm violence occurred in schools.

[2]The fatal data from the National Vital Statistics System does not have victim-offender relationship information. The SHR victim-offender relationship data are not shown due to the large amount of missing data.

TABLE 6
Nonfatal firearm and nonfirearm violence, by victim-offender relationship, 2007–2011

Relationship to victim	Total nonfatal violence	Firearm violence		Nonfirearm violence	
		Number	Percent of total violence	Number	Percent of total violence
Total	29,611,300	2,218,500	7.5%	27,392,800	92.5%
Nonstranger	15,715,900	738,000	4.7	14,977,900	95.3
Intimate[a]	4,673,600	195,700	4.2	4,477,900	95.8
Other relative	2,157,700	158,100	7.3	1,999,500	92.7
Friend/acquaintance	8,884,600	384,100	4.3	8,500,500	95.7
Stranger	10,983,100	1,177,900	10.7	9,805,200	89.3
Unknown[b]	2,912,300	302,600	10.4	2,609,600	89.6

Note: Detail may not sum to total due to rounding. See appendix table 17 for standard errors.
[a]Includes current or former spouses, boyfriends, or girlfriends.
[b]Includes relationships unknown and number of offenders unknown.
Source: Bureau of Justice Statistics, National Crime Victimization Survey, 2007–2011.

TABLE 7
Nonfatal firearm and nonfirearm violence, by location of crime, 2007–2011

Location	Total nonfatal violence		Firearm violence		Nonfirearm violence	
	Number	Percent	Number	Percent	Number	Percent
Total	29,618,300	100%	2,218,500	100%	27,399,800	100%
Victims home or lodging	6,491,400	21.9	427,600	19.3	6,063,800	22.1
Near victim's home	4,804,700	16.2	504,500	22.7	4,300,200	15.7
In, at, or near a friend, neighbor, or relative's home	2,175,900	7.3	132,600	6.0	2,043,300	7.5
Commercial place	2,878,600	9.7	195,400	8.8	2,683,200	9.8
Parking lot or garage	1,688,400	5.7	340,600	15.4	1,347,900	4.9
School*	3,931,100	13.3	12,600 !	0.6 !	3,918,500	14.3
Open area, on street, or public transportation	4,636,900	15.7	508,400	22.9	4,128,500	15.1
Other location	3,011,200	10.2	96,800	4.4	2,914,400	10.6

! Interpret with caution. Estimate based on 10 or fewer sample cases, or coefficient of variation is greater than 50%. See appendix table 18 for standard errors.
*Includes inside a school building or on school property.
Source: Bureau of Justice Statistics, National Crime Victimization Survey, 2007–2011.

School-related homicides of youth ages 5 to 18 accounted for less than 2% of all youth homicides

The number of homicides at schools declined over time, from an average of 29 per year in the 1990s (school year 1992-93 to 1999-00) to an average of 20 per year in the 2000s (school year 2000-01 to 2009-10) (table 8). Generally, homicides in schools comprised less than 2% of all homicides of youth ages 5 to 18. During the 2000s, an average of about 1,600 homicides of youth ages 5 to 18 occurred per year. The majority of homicides against youth both at school and away from school were committed with a firearm.

TABLE 8

School-associated homicides of youth ages 5 to 18, by location and school years, 1992–93 to 2009–10

School year	Homicides of youth ages 5 to 18		
	Total homicides[a]	Homicides at school[b,c]	Percent of all homicides of youth at school
1992–93	2,719	34	1.3%
1993–94	2,911	29	1.0
1994–95	2,691	28	1.0
1995–96	2,548	32	1.3
1996–97	2,210	28	1.3
1997–98	2,104	34	1.6
1998–99	1,791	33	1.8
1999–00	1,566	14	0.9
2000–01	1,501	14	0.9
2001–02	1,494	16	1.1
2002–03	1,538	18	1.2
2003–04	1,459	23	1.6
2004–05	1,545	22	1.4
2005–06	1,687	21	1.2
2006–07	1,796	32	1.8
2007–08	1,740	21	1.2
2008–09	1,579	17	1.1
2009–10	…	17	…

Note: At school includes on school property, on the way to or from regular sessions at school, and while attending or traveling to or from a school-sponsored event.

…Not available.

[a]Youth ages 5 to 18 from July 1, 1992, through June 30, 2009.

[b]Youth ages 5 to 18 from July 1, 1992, through June 30, 2010.

[c]The data from school year 1999–00 through 2009–10 are subject to change until interviews with school and law enforcement officials have been completed. The details learned during the interviews can occasionally change the classification of a case.

Sources: Table 1.1 from Robers, S., Zhang, J., and Truman, J. (2012). *Indicators of School Crime and Safety: 2011* (NCES 2012-002/NCJ 236021). National Center for Education Statistics, U.S. Department of Education, and Bureau of Justice Statistics, Office of Justice Programs, U.S. Department of Justice. Homicide data are from: Centers for Disease Control and Prevention (CDC), 1992–2010 School-Associated Violent Deaths Surveillance Study (SAVD); FBI and Supplementary Homicide Reports (SHR), 1992–2009.

In 2007-11, about 23% of all nonfatal firearm victims were injured

In 2007-11, about 23% of all nonfatal firearm victims were physically injured during the victimization (table 9). About 7% suffered serious injuries (e.g., a gunshot wound, broken bone, or internal injuries), while 16% suffered minor injuries (e.g., bruises or cuts). Of the nonfatal firearm victims who were injured, 72% received some type of care, with about 82% receiving care in a hospital or medical office.

The victim reported that the offender had fired the weapon in 7% of all nonfatal firearm victimizations. The victim suffered a gunshot wound in 28% of these victimizations (not shown in table).

TABLE 9
Nonfatal firearm and nonfirearm violence, by injury and treatment received, 2007–2011

Injury and treatment	Total nonfatal violence		Firearm violence		Nonfirearm violence	
	Number	Percent	Number	Percent	Number	Percent
Injury	29,618,300	100%	2,218,500	100%	27,399,800	100%
Not injured	22,187,500	74.9	1,707,800	77.0	20,479,700	74.7
Injured	7,430,800	25.1	510,700	23.0	6,920,100	25.3
Serious[a]	1,249,300	4.2	148,300	6.7	1,147,000	4.2
Gun shot	46,000	0.2	46,000	2.1	~	~
Minor[b]	5,742,700	19.4	357,100	16.1	5,385,700	19.7
Rape without other injuries	374,300	1.3	5,400 !	0.2 !	368,900	1.3
Treatment for injury[c]	7,430,800	100%	510,700	100%	6,920,100	100%
No treatment	4,304,300	57.9	140,700	27.5	4,163,600	60.2
Any treatment	3,103,500	41.8	370,000	72.5	2,733,500	39.5
Treatment setting[d]	3,103,500	100%	370,000	100%	2,733,500	100%
At the scene/home of victim, neighbor, or friend/location	1,078,000	34.7	68,000	18.4	1,010,000	36.9
In doctor's office/hospital emergency room/ overnight at hospital	2,025,600	65.3	302,000	81.6	1,723,500	63.1

Note: See appendix table 19 for standard errors.
! Interpret with caution. Estimate based on 10 or fewer sample cases, or coefficient of variation is greater than 50%.
~Not applicable.
[a]Includes injuries such as gun shots, knife wounds, internal injuries, unconsciousness, and broken bones.
[b]Includes bruises, cuts, and other minor injuries.
[c]Includes only victims who were injured.
[d]Includes only victims who were injured and received treatment.
Source: Bureau of Justice Statistics, National Crime Victimization Survey, 2007–2011.

Nonfatal shooting victims

According to the NCVS, an average of about 22,000 nonfatal shooting victims occurred annually from 1993 to 2002 (not shown in table). From 2002 to 2011, the number of victims declined by about half to 12,900 per year. In the 5-year aggregate period from 2007-11, a total of 46,000 nonfatal firearm victims were wounded with a firearm and another 58,483 were victims of a firearm homicide. The total firearm nonfatal gunshot injuries and homicides accounted for 5% of all firearm violent crimes in 2007-11.

Data on nonfatal injury are also available in the National Electronic Injury Surveillance System All Injury Program (NEISS-AIP), which is operated by the U.S. Consumer Product Safety Commission (CPSC). According to these data, an average of 47,870 nonfatal assault injuries resulted from a firearm from 2001 to 2011 (figure 11). In 2007-11, the average number of nonfatal injuries from a firearm increased slightly to 51,810.

The differences noted between the NCVS and NEISS-AIP firearm injury estimates are due in part to a variety of technical issues. Both estimates are generated from samples and are subject to sampling error. The NCVS is a residential household survey that does not include the homeless, persons in institutional settings such as jails, prisons, mental health facilities, and certain other group quarters. Therefore, NCVS may miss injuries that involve persons who are homeless, victims who require lengthy stays in a hospital, and offenders who are incarcerated or placed in other institutional settings after the incident.

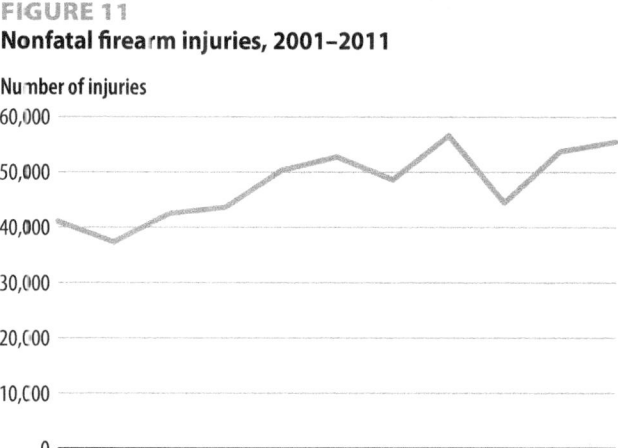

FIGURE 11

Nonfatal firearm injuries, 2001–2011

Number of injuries

Note: See appendix table 20 for numbers and standard errors.

! Interpret with caution. Estimate based on fewer than 20 NEISS cases (based on unweighted data), national estimates less than 1,200 (based on weighted data), or the coefficient of variation (CV) of the estimate greater than 30%.

Source: Consumer Product Safety Commission, National Electronic Injury Surveillance System All Injury Program (NEISS-AIP), 2001–2011. Accessed from the National Center for Injury Prevention and Control, CDC.

The majority of firearm violence is reported to the police

In 2007-11, about 61% of nonfatal firearm violence was reported to the police, compared to 46% of nonfirearm violence (table 10). Among the nonfatal firearm victimizations that went unreported in 2007-11, the most common reasons victims gave for not reporting the crime was fear of reprisal (31%) and that the police could not or would not do anything to help (27%).

In 2007-11, about 1% of nonfatal violent crime victims used a firearm in self defense

In 2007-11, there were 235,700 victimizations where the victim used a firearm to threaten or attack an offender (table 11). This amounted to approximately 1% of all nonfatal violent victimizations in the 5-year period. The percentage of nonfatal violent victimizations involving firearm use in self defense remained stable at under 2% from 1993 to 2011 (not shown in table). In 2007-11, about 44% of victims of nonfatal violent crime offered no resistance, 1% attacked or threatened the offender with another type of weapon, 22% attacked or threatened without a weapon (e.g., hit or kicked), and 26% used nonconfrontational methods (e.g., yelling, running, hiding, or arguing).

In instances where the victim was armed with a firearm, the offender was also armed with a gun in 32% of the victimizations, compared to 63% of victimizations where the offender was armed with a lesser weapon, such as a knife, or unarmed (not shown in table). A small number of property crime victims also used a firearm in self defense (103,000 victims or about 0.1% of all property victimizations); however, the majority of victims (86%) were not present during the incident. No information was available on the number of homicide victims that attempted to defend themselves with a firearm or by other means.

TABLE 10

Nonfatal firearm and nonfirearm violence reported and not reported to police, 2007–2011

	Total nonfatal violence	Firearm violence	Nonfirearm violence
Total	100%	100%	100%
Reported	46.9%	61.5%	45.7%
Not reported	51.7%	37.6%	52.9%
Reason not reported	100%	100%	100%
Dealt with it another way	35.0	12.1	36.4
Not important enough to respondent	18.4	6.2	19.1
Police could not or would not help	16.7	27.1	16.1
Fear of reprisal	6.5	31.3	5.1
Did not want to get offender in trouble advised not to report	5.1	4.3 !	5.1
Other/unknown/not one most important reason	18.2	19.0	18.2

Note: Detail may not sum to total due to rounding. Reasons for not reporting represent the reason the victim stated was most important. See appendix table 21 for standard errors.

!Interpret with caution. Estimate based on 10 or fewer sample cases, or coefficient of variation is greater than 50%.

Source: Bureau of Justice Statistics, National Crime Victimization Survey, 2007–2011.

TABLE 11

Self-protective behaviors, by type of crime, 2007–2011

Self-protective behavior	Violent crime		Property crime	
	Number	Percent	Number	Percent
Total	29,618,300	100%	84,495,500	100%
Offered no resistance	12,987,300	43.8	10,162,000	12.0
Threatened or attacked with a firearm	235,700	0.8	103,000	0.1
Threatened or attacked with other weapon	391,100	1.3	38,200	--
Threatened or attacked without a weapon	6,552,900	22.1	421,300	0.5
Nonconfrontational tactics[a]	7,768,700	26.2	1,187,100	1.4
Other	1,641,300	5.5	223,400	0.3
Unknown	41,300	0.1	12,200 !	--
Victim was not present[b]	~	~	72,348,200	85.6

Note: See appendix table 22 for standard errors.

! Interpret with caution. Estimate based on 10 or fewer sample cases, or coefficient of variation is greater than 50%.

~Not applicable.

--Less than 0.05%.

[a]Includes yelling, running, or arguing.

[b]Includes property crime where the victim was not present.

Source: Bureau of Justice Statistics, National Crime Victimization Survey, 2007–2011.

Firearm use by offenders

In 2004, an estimated 16% of state prison inmates and 18% of federal inmates reported that they used, carried, or possessed a firearm when they committed the crime for which they were serving a prison sentence (table 12). This represented a slight change from 1997, where an estimated 18% of state prison inmates and 16% of federal inmates reported having a firearm when they committed the crime for their current sentence. During the offense that brought them to prison, 13% of state inmates and 16% of federal inmates carried a handgun. In addition, about 1% had a rifle and another 2% had a shotgun. Of inmates armed with a firearm during the offense, about 7% of state inmates and 8% of federal inmates were armed with either a single shot firearm or a conventional semiautomatic, and 2% of state inmates and 3% of federal inmates were armed with a military-style semiautomatic or fully automatic firearm (table 13).

In 2004, among state prison inmates who possessed a gun at the time of offense, fewer than 2% bought their firearm at a flea market or gun show, about 10% purchased it from a retail store or pawnshop, 37% obtained it from family or friends, and another 40% obtained it from an illegal source (table 14). This was similar to the percentage distribution in 1997.

TABLE 12
Possession of firearms by state and federal prison inmates at time of offense, by type of firearm, 1997 and 2004

Type of firearm	1997		2004	
	State	Federal	State	Federal
Total	100%	100%	100%	100%
Firearm	18.3%	15.8%	15.8%	17.8%
Handgun	15.1	13.6	13.3	15.5
Rifle	1.3	1.4	1.3	1.5
Shotgun	2.3	2.1	1.7	2.0
Other	0.4	0.5	0.1	0.1
No firearm	81.7%	84.2%	84.2%	82.2%

Note: Includes only inmates with a current conviction. Estimates may differ from previously published BJS reports. To account for differences in the 1997 and 2004 inmate survey questionnaires, the analytical methodology used in 1997 was revised to ensure comparability with the 2004 survey. Detail may not sum to total as inmates may have had possessed more than one firearm.

Source: Bureau of Justice Statistics, Survey of Inmates in State and Federal Correctional Facilities, 1997 and 2004.

TABLE 13
Possession of firearms by state and federal prison inmates at time of offense, by specific type of firearm, 1997 and 2004

Specific type of firearm	1997		2004	
	State	Federal	State	Federal
Single shot	9.9%	7.6%	7.5%	8.2%
Conventional semiautomatic	7.8	8.3	6.6	7.9
Military-style semiautomatic or fully automatic	1.5	1.7	2.0	3.2
Other	0.1	0.2	0.1	0.1

Note: Includes only inmates with a current conviction. Estimates may differ from previously published BJS reports. To account for differences in the 1997 and 2004 inmate survey questionnaires, the analytical methodology used in 1997 was revised to ensure comparability with the 2004 survey.

Source: Bureau of Justice Statistics, Survey of Inmates in State and Federal Correctional Facilities, 1997 and 2004.

TABLE 14
Source of firearms possessed by state prison inmates at time of offense, 1997 and 2004

Source of firearm	Percent of state prison inmates	
	1997	2004
Total	100%	100%
Purchased or traded from—	14.0%	11.3%
Retail store	8.2	7.3
Pawnshop	4.0	2.6
Flea market	1.0	0.6
Gun show	0.8	0.8
Family or friend	40.1%	37.4%
Purchased or traded	12.6	12.2
Rented or borrowed	18.9	14.1
Other	8.5	11.1
Street/illegal source	37.3%	40.0%
Theft or burglary	9.1	7.5
Drug dealer/off street	20.3	25.2
Fence/black market	8.0	7.4
Other	8.7%	11.2%

Note: Includes only inmates with a current conviction. Estimates may differ from previously published BJS reports. To account for differences in the 1997 and 2004 inmate survey questionnaires, the analytical methodology used in 1997 was revised to ensure comparability with the 2004 survey.

Source: Bureau of Justice Statistics, Survey of Inmates in State and Federal Correctional Facilities, 1997 and 2004.

Methodology

Estimates in this report are based primarily on data from the Bureau of Justice Statistics' (BJS) National Crime Victimization Survey (NCVS) and the National Center for Health Statistics' (NCHS) Centers for Disease Control and Prevention Center for Disease Control's Web-based Injury Statistics Query and Reporting System (WISQARS). Additional estimates come from the School-Associated Violent Deaths Surveillance Study (SAVD), the National Electronic Injury Surveillance System All Injury Program (NEISS-AIP) data, the FBI's Supplemental Homicide Reports (SHR), the Survey of Inmates in State Correctional Facilities (SISCF), and the Survey of Inmates in Federal Correctional Facilities (SIFCF).

The National Crime Victimization Survey (NCVS)

The NCVS is an annual data collection conducted by the U.S. Census Bureau for BJS. The NCVS is a self-report survey in which interviewed persons are asked about the number and characteristics of victimizations experienced during the prior 6 months. The NCVS collects information on nonfatal personal crimes (rape or sexual assault, robbery, aggravated assault, simple assault, and personal larceny) and household property crimes (burglary, motor vehicle theft, and other theft) both reported and not reported to police. In addition to providing annual level and change estimates on criminal victimization, the NCVS is the primary source of information on the nature of criminal victimization incidents. Survey respondents provide information about themselves (such as age, sex, race and ethnicity, marital status, education level, and income) and if they experienced a victimization. For crime victims, data are collected about each victimization incident, including information about the offender (such as age, race and ethnicity, sex, and victim-offender relationship), characteristics of the crime (including time and place of occurrence, use of weapons, nature of injury, and economic consequences), whether the crime was reported to police, reasons why the crime was or was not reported, and experiences with the criminal justice system.

The NCVS is administered to persons age 12 or older from a nationally representative sample of households in the United States. In 2011, about 143,120 persons age 12 or older from 79,800 households across the country were interviewed during the year. Once selected, households remain in the sample for 3 years, and eligible persons in these households are interviewed every 6 months for a total of seven interviews. New households rotate into the sample on an ongoing basis to replace outgoing households that have been in sample for the 3-year period. The sample includes persons living in group quarters (such as dormitories, rooming houses, and religious group dwellings) and excludes persons living in military barracks and institutional settings (such as correctional or hospital facilities) and the homeless. (For more information, see the *Survey Methodology for Criminal Victimization in the United States, 2008*, NCJ 231173, BJS website, May 2011.)

The 79,800 households that participated in the NCVS in 2011 represent a 90% household response rate. The person level response rate—the percentage of persons age 12 or older in participating households who completed an NCVS interview—was 88% in 2011.

For this report, prior to applying the weights to the data, all victimizations that occurred outside of the U.S. were excluded. From 1993 to 2011, less than 1% of the unweighted violent victimizations occurred outside of the U.S. and was excluded from the analyses.

Weighting adjustments for estimating personal victimization

Estimates in this report use data primarily from the 1993 to 2011 NCVS data files weighted to produce annual estimates for persons age 12 or older living in U.S. households. Because the NCVS relies on a sample rather than a census of the entire U.S. population, weights are designed to inflate sample point estimates to known population totals and to compensate for survey nonresponse and other aspects of the sample design.

The NCVS data files include both household and person weights. The household weight is commonly used to calculate estimates of property crimes, such as motor vehicle theft or burglary, which are identified with the household. Person weights provide an estimate of the population represented by each person in the sample. Person weights are most frequently used to compute estimates of crime victimizations of persons in the total population. Both household and person weights, after proper adjustment, are also used to form the denominator in calculations of crime rates.

The victimization weights used in this analysis account for the number of persons present during an incident and for repeat victims of series incidents. The weight counts series incidents as the actual number of incidents reported by the victim, up to a maximum of ten incidents. Series victimizations are victimizations that are similar in type but occur with such frequency that a victim is unable to recall each individual event or to describe each event in detail. Survey procedures allow NCVS interviewers to identify and classify these similar victimizations as series victimizations and collect detailed information on only the most recent incident in the series. In 2011, about 2% of all victimizations were series incidents. Weighting series incidents as the number of incidents up to a maximum of ten produces more reliable estimates of crime levels, while the cap at ten minimizes the effect of extreme outliers on the rates. Additional information on the series enumeration is detailed in *Methods for Counting High Frequency Repeat Victimizations in the National Crime Victimization Survey*, NCJ 237308, BJS website, April 2012.

Standard error computations

When national estimates are derived from a sample, as is the case with the NCVS, caution must be taken when comparing one estimate to another estimate or when comparing estimates over time. Although one estimate may be larger than another, estimates based on a sample have some degree of sampling error. The sampling error of an estimate depends on several factors, including the amount of variation in the responses, the size of the sample, and the size of the subgroup for which the estimate is computed. When the sampling error around the estimates is taken into consideration, the estimates that appear different may, in fact, not be statistically different.

One measure of the sampling error associated with an estimate is the standard error. The standard error can vary from one estimate to the next. In general, for a given metric, an estimate with a smaller standard error provides a more reliable approximation of the true value than an estimate with a larger standard error. Estimates with relatively large standard errors are associated with less precision and reliability and should be interpreted with caution.

In order to generate standard errors around estimates from the NCVS, the Census Bureau produces generalized variance function (GVF) parameters for BJS. The GVFs take into account aspects of the NCVS complex sample design and represent the curve fitted to a selection of individual standard errors based on the Jackknife Repeated Replication technique. The GVF parameters were used to generate standard errors for each point estimate (such as counts, percentages, and rates) in the report. For average annual estimates, standard errors were based on the ratio of the sums of victimizations and respondents across years.

In this report, BJS conducted tests to determine whether differences in estimated numbers and percentages were statistically significant once sampling error was taken into account. Using statistical programs developed specifically for the NCVS, all comparisons in the text were tested for significance. The primary test procedure used was Student's t-statistic, which tests the difference between two sample estimates. To ensure that the observed differences between estimates were larger than might be expected due to sampling variation, the significance level was set at the 95% confidence level.

Data users can use the estimates and the standard errors of the estimates provided in this report to generate a confidence interval around the estimate as a measure of the margin of error. The following example illustrates how standard errors can be used to generate confidence intervals:

> According to the NCVS, in 2011, the rate of nonfatal firearm violence was 1.8 per 1,000 (see table 1). Using the GVFs, BJS determined that the estimate has a standard error of 0.2 (see appendix table 3). A confidence interval around the estimate was generated by multiplying the standard errors by ±1.96 (the t-score of a normal, two-tailed distribution that excludes 2.5% at either end of the distribution). Thus, the confidence interval around the 1.8 estimate from 2011 is 1.8 ± 0.2 (0.2 X 1.96) or (1.4 to 2.2). In other words, if different samples using the same procedures were taken from the U.S. population in 2011, 95% of the time the rate of nonfatal firearm violence was between 1.4 and 2.2 per 1,000.

In this report, BJS also calculated a coefficient of variation (CV) for all estimates, representing the ratio of the standard error to the estimate. CVs provide a measure of reliability and a means to compare the precision of estimates across measures with differing levels or metrics. If the CV was greater than 50%, or the unweighted sample had 10 or fewer cases, the estimate would have been noted with a "!" symbol (interpret data with caution; estimate is based on 10 or fewer sample cases, or the coefficient of variation exceeds 50%).

Many of the variables examined in this report may be related to one another and to other variables not included in the analyses. Complex relationships among variables were not fully explored in this report and warrant more extensive analysis. Readers are cautioned not to draw causal inferences based on the results presented.

Methodological changes to the NCVS in 2006

Methodological changes implemented in 2006 may have affected the crime estimates for that year to such an extent that they are not comparable to estimates from other years. Evaluation of 2007 and later data from the NCVS conducted by BJS and the Census Bureau found a high degree of confidence that estimates for 2007, 2008, 2009, and 2010 are consistent with and comparable to estimates for 2005 and previous years. The reports, *Criminal Victimization, 2006*, NCJ 219413, December 2007; *Criminal Victimization, 2007*, NCJ 224390, December 2008; *Criminal Victimization, 2008*, NCJ 227777, September 2009; *Criminal Victimization, 2009*, NCJ 231327, October 2010; *Criminal Victimization, 2010*, NCJ 235508, September 2011; and *Criminal Victimization, 2011*, NCJ 239437, October 2012, are available on the BJS website.

Although caution is warranted when comparing data from 2006 to other years, the aggregation of multiple years of data in this report diminishes the potential variation between 2006 and other years. In general, findings do not change significantly if data for 2006 are excluded from the analyses.

Web-based Injury Statistics Query and Reporting System Fatal (WISQARS™ Fatal)

WISQARS Fatal provides mortality data related to injury. The mortality data reported in WISQARS Fatal come from death certificate data reported to the CDC's National Center for Health Statistics (NCHS). Data include causes of death reported by attending physicians, medical examiners, and coroners. It also includes demographic information about decedents reported by funeral directors, who obtain that information from family members and other informants. NCHS collects, compiles, verifies, and prepares these data for release to the public. The data provide information about what types of injuries are leading causes of deaths, how common they are, and who they affect. These data are intended for a broad audience—the public, the media, public health practitioners and researchers, and public health officials—to increase their knowledge of injury.

WISQARS Fatal mortality reports provide tables of the total numbers of injury-related deaths and the death rates per 100,000 U.S. population. The reports list deaths according to cause (mechanism) and intent (manner) of injury by state, race, Hispanic origin, sex, and age groupings. Data in this report are provided for homicides by firearm from 1993 to 2010, including some preliminary 2011 estimates. The injury mortality data were classified based on the International Classification of Diseases (ICD)-10 classification system from 1999 and later, and the ICD-9 system for 1998 and earlier. The comparability study showed that the comparability for homicide and firearm homicide between the two systems was very high; therefore, data are shown from both periods.[3]

National Electronic Injury Surveillance System All Injury Program (NEISS-AIP)

The NEISS-AIP is operated by the U.S. Consumer Product Safety Commission (CPSC). It is a collaborative effort by the National Center for Injury Prevention and Control (NCIPC) and CPSC. The NEISS is a national probability sample of hospitals in the U.S. and its territories. Data are collected about all types and external causes of nonfatal injuries and poisonings treated in U.S. hospital emergency departments, whether or not they are associated with consumer products. This report uses the estimates on nonfatal assault injuries from a firearm. This excludes injuries that were unintentional, by legal intervention, or self-harm.

---

[3]National Center for Health Statistics. (2001). Comparability of cause of death between ICD-9 and ICD-10: Preliminary estimates. Retrieved from http://www.cdc.gov/nchs/data/nvsr/nvsr49/nvsr49_02.pdf.

School-Associated Violent Deaths Surveillance Study (SAVD)

The SAVD is an epidemiological study developed by the Centers for Disease Control and Prevention in conjunction with the U.S. Department of Education and the U.S. Department of Justice. SAVD seeks to describe the epidemiology of school-associated violent deaths, identify common features of these deaths, estimate the rate of school-associated violent death in the United States, and identify potential risk factors for these deaths. The surveillance system includes descriptive data on all school-associated violent deaths in the United States, including all homicides, suicides, or legal intervention in which the fatal injury occurred on the campus of a functioning elementary or secondary school; while the victim was on the way to or from regular sessions at such a school; or while attending or on the way to or from an official school-sponsored event. Victims of such incidents include nonstudents, as well as students and staff members. SAVD includes descriptive information about the school, event, victim(s), and offender(s). The SAVD Surveillance System has collected data from July 1, 1992, through the present.

SAVD uses a four-step process to identify and collect data on school-associated violent deaths. Cases are initially identified through a search of the LexisNexis newspaper and media database. Then law enforcement officials are contacted to confirm the details of the case and to determine if the event meets the case definition. Once a case is confirmed, a law enforcement official and a school official are interviewed regarding details about the school, event, victim(s), and offender(s). A copy of the full law enforcement report is also sought for each case. The information obtained on schools includes school demographics, attendance/absentee rates, suspensions/expulsions and mobility, school history of weapon-carrying incidents, security measures, violence prevention activities, school response to the event, and school policies about weapon carrying. Event information includes the location of injury, the context of injury (e.g., while classes were being held or during break), motives for injury, method of injury, and school and community events happening around the time period. Information obtained on victim(s) and offender(s) includes demographics, circumstances of the event (date/time, alcohol or drug use, and number of persons involved), types and origins of weapons, criminal history, psychological risk factors, school-related problems, extracurricular activities, and family history, including structure and stressors.

For several reasons, all data from 1999 to the present are flagged as preliminary. For some recent data, the interviews with school and law enforcement officials to verify case details have not been completed. The details learned during the interviews can occasionally change the classification of a case. Also, new cases may be identified because of the expansion of the scope of the media files used for case identification. Sometimes other cases not identified during earlier data years using the independent case finding efforts (which focus on nonmedia sources of information) will be discovered. Also, other cases may occasionally be identified while the law enforcement and school interviews are being conducted to verify known cases.

The FBI's Uniform Crime Reporting (UCR) Program, Supplementary Homicide Reports (SHR)

The FBI's SHR were used for information about gun type used in firearm homicides. The UCR program collects and publishes criminal offense, arrest, and law enforcement personnel statistics. Under the UCR program, law enforcement agencies submit information to the FBI monthly. Offense information is collected on the eight Part I offenses: homicide, forcible rape, robbery, aggravated assault, burglary, larceny-theft, motor vehicle theft, and arson. The UCR program collects data on only those crimes that come to the attention of law enforcement.

Homicide incident information—through SHR data—is submitted with details on location, victim, and offender characteristics. Homicide is defined as murder and non-negligent manslaughter, which is the willful killing of one human being by another. The analyses excludes deaths caused by negligence, suicide, or accident; justifiable homicides; and attempts to murder. Deaths from the terrorist attacks of September 11, 2001, are not included in any of the analyses.

Not all agencies that report offense information to the FBI also submit supplemental data on homicides. About 90 percent of homicides are included in the SHR. However, adjustments can be made to the weights to correct for missing victim reports. Estimates from the SHR used in this report were generated by BJS using a weight developed by BJS that reconciles the counts of SHR homicide victims with those in the UCR for the 1992 through 2011 data years.

Surveys of Inmates in State and Federal Correctional Facilities (SISCF and SIFCF)

The SISCF and the SIFCF have provided nationally representative data on state prison inmates and sentenced federal inmates held in federally owned and operated facilities. The SISCF was conducted in 1974, 1979, 1986, 1991, 1997, and 2004, and the SIFCF in 1991, 1997, and 2004. The 2004 SISCF was conducted for BJS by the U.S. Census Bureau, which also conducted the SIFCF for BJS and the Federal Bureau of Prisons. Both surveys provide information about current offense and criminal history, family background and personal characteristics, prior drug and alcohol use and treatment, gun possession, and prison treatment, programs, and services. The surveys are the only national source of detailed information on criminal offenders, particularly special populations such as drug and alcohol users and offenders who have mental health problems. Systematic random sampling was used to select the inmates, and the 2004 surveys of state and federal inmates were administered through CAPI. In 2004, 14,499 state prisoners in 287 state prisons and 3,686 federal prisoners in 39 federal prisons were interviewed.

APPENDIX TABLE 1
Numbers and rates for figure 1: Firearm homicides, 1993–2011

Year	Number	Rate per 100,000 persons
1993	18,253	7.0
1994	17,527	6.7
1995	15,551	5.8
1996	14,037	5.2
1997	13,252	4.9
1998	11,798	4.3
1999	10,828	3.9
2000	10,801	3.8
2001	11,348	4.0
2002	11,829	4.1
2003	11,920	4.1
2004	11,624	4.0
2005	12,352	4.2
2006	12,791	4.3
2007	12,632	4.2
2008	12,179	4.0
2009	11,493	3.8
2010	11,078	3.6
2011	11,101	3.6

Source: Centers for Disease Control and Prevention, National Center for Injury Prevention and Control. Web-based Injury Statistics Query and Reporting System (WISQARS), 1993–2010. Retrieved March 2013 from www.cdc.gov/ncipc/wisqars.

APPENDIX TABLE 2
Numbers, rates, and standard errors for figure 2: Nonfatal firearm victimizations, 1993–2011

	Number	Standard error	Rate per 1,000 persons age 12 or older	Standard error
1993	1,529,700	104,582	7.3	0.5
1994	1,568,200	83,431	7.4	0.4
1995	1,193,200	70,572	5.5	0.3
1996	1,100,800	68,653	5.1	0.3
1997	1,024,100	72,643	4.7	0.3
1998	835,400	69,401	3.8	0.3
1999	640,900	54,713	2.9	0.2
2000	610,200	55,220	2.7	0.2
2001	563,100	53,309	2.5	0.2
2002	540,000	50,299	2.3	0.2
2003	467,300	47,783	2.0	0.2
2004	456,500	47,513	1.9	0.2
2005	503,500	55,594	2.1	0.2
2006	614,400	61,310	2.5	0.2
2007	554,800	55,886	2.2	0.2
2008	371,300	45,794	1.5	0.2
2009	410,100	48,765	1.6	0.2
2010	415,000	47,172	1.6	0.2
2011	467,300	53,197	1.8	0.2

Source: Bureau of Justice Statistics, National Crime Victimization Survey, 1993–2011.

Standard errors for table 1: Criminal firearm violence, 1993–2011

Year	Total fatal and nonfatal firearm violence	Number		Rate of nonfatal firearm victimization	Percent of all violence involving firearms
		Nonfatal firearm victimizations	Nonfatal firearm incidents		
1993	105,349	104,582	91,169	0.5	0.6%
1994	84,005	83,431	73,911	0.4	0.4
1995	71,131	70,572	64,501	0.3	0.4
1996	69,183	68,653	62,377	0.3	0.5
1997	73,220	72,643	66,331	0.3	0.5
1998	70,022	69,401	60,556	0.3	0.5
1999	55,268	54,713	48,457	0.2	0.5
2000	55,810	55,220	48,015	0.2	0.6
2001	53,967	53,309	49,987	0.2	0.7
2002	50,946	50,299	45,234	0.2	0.6
2003	48,494	47,783	42,668	0.2	0.6
2004	48,200	47,513	44,433	0.2	0.7
2005	56,378	55,594	51,864	0.2	0.8
2006	62,038	61,310	57,669	0.2	0.7
2007	56,652	55,886	49,166	0.2	0.8
2008	46,637	45,794	42,966	0.2	0.7
2009	49,561	48,765	46,881	0.2	0.8
2010	47,913	47,172	44,695	0.2	0.9
2011	53,942	53,197	49,563	0.2	0.8

~Not applicable.

Source: Bureau of Justice Statistics, National Crime Victimization Survey, 1993–2011.

Standard errors for table 2: Percent of violence involving a firearm, by type of crime, 1993–2011

Year	Nonfatal violence	Robbery	Aggravated assault
1993	0.6%	2.2%	1.9%
1994	0.4	1.9	1.5
1995	0.4	2.1	1.5
1996	0.4	2.0	1.5
1997	0.5	2.2	1.7
1998	0.5	2.5	1.9
1999	0.5	2.3	1.8
2000	0.6	2.6	2.2
2001	0.6	3.4	2.3
2002	0.6	3.2	2.5
2003	0.6	3.1	2.3
2004	0.7	3.2	2.4
2005	0.8	3.3	2.8
2006	0.7	2.7	2.4
2007	0.8	2.9	2.9
2008	0.7	3.3	3.1
2009	0.8	3.8	2.9
2010	0.9	3.7	3.1
2011	0.8	4.0	3.2

Source: Bureau of Justice Statistics, National Crime Victimization Survey, 1993–2011.

APPENDIX TABLE 5
Standard errors for table 3: Criminal firearm violence, by type of firearm, 1994–2011

Year	Handgun		Other firearm		Gun type unknown	
	Number	Percent	Number	Percent	Number	Percent
1994	94,313	1.8%	26,713	1.6%	6,951	0.4%
1995	77,109	1.6	21,832	1.5	4,899	0.4
1996	66,253	1.9	21,995	1.8	4,366	0.4
1997	68,335	2.3	25,950	2.2	5,534	0.5
1998	68,151	2.6	25,521	2.5	4,522	0.5
1999	63,909	2.5	18,379	2.3	4,189	0.6
2000	57,439	2.8	17,323	2.6	4,260	0.7
2001	53,625	3.1	17,115	2.7	7,586	1.3
2002	48,977	3.1	16,006	2.7	7,929	1.4
2003	46,655	3.2	14,670	2.7	7,392	1.4
2004	45,846	3.6	15,535	3.1	8,509	1.8
2005	50,621	3.8	17,269	3.3	8,153	1.7
2006	56,341	3.1	15,872	2.7	8,415	1.5
2007	56,630	3.2	18,308	2.9	6,598	1.1
2008	48,199	3.6	16,622	3.3	4,666	1.0
2009	47,110	3.7	14,157	3.4	4,688	1.2
2010	50,636	3.1	11,837	2.7	4,313	1.0
2011	43,185	3.1	13,868	2.9	2,676	0.6

Source: Bureau of Justice Statistics, National Crime Victimization Survey, 1993–2011.

APPENDIX TABLE 6
Numbers and rates for figure 3: Firearm homicides, by sex, 1993–2010

Year	Number		Rate per 100,000 persons	
	Male	Female	Male	Female
1993	15,228	3,025	12.0	2.3
1994	14,766	2,761	11.5	2.1
1995	13,021	2,530	10.0	1.9
1996	11,735	2,302	8.9	1.7
1997	11,147	2,105	8.4	1.5
1998	9,771	2,027	7.2	1.4
1999	8,944	1,884	6.5	1.3
2000	9,006	1,795	6.5	1.3
2001	9,532	1,816	6.8	1.3
2002	9,899	1,930	7.0	1.3
2003	10,126	1,794	7.1	1.2
2004	9,921	1,703	6.9	1.1
2005	10,561	1,791	7.3	1.2
2006	10,886	1,905	7.4	1.3
2007	10,767	1,865	7.3	1.2
2008	10,361	1,818	6.9	1.2
2009	9,615	1,878	6.4	1.2
2010	9,340	1,738	6.2	1.1

Source: Centers for Disease Control and Prevention, National Center for Injury Prevention and Control. Web-based Injury Statistics Query and Reporting System (WISQARS), 1993–2010. Retrieved March 2013 from www.cdc.gov/ncipc/wisqars.

APPENDIX TABLE 7
Rates and standard errors for figure 4: Nonfatal firearm violence, by sex, 1994–2011

Year	Male		Female	
	Rate*	Standard error	Rate*	Standard error
1994	10.1	0.6	4.7	0.4
1995	9.3	0.5	3.7	0.3
1996	7.6	0.4	3.1	0.2
1997	6.4	0.4	3.5	0.3
1998	5.5	0.4	3.0	0.3
1999	4.4	0.4	2.3	0.2
2000	3.7	0.3	1.9	0.2
2001	3.5	0.3	1.7	0.2
2002	2.9	0.3	1.9	0.2
2003	2.7	0.2	1.6	0.2
2004	2.5	0.2	1.4	0.2
2005	2.5	0.3	1.4	0.2
2006	2.8	0.3	1.8	0.2
2007	2.8	0.3	1.9	0.2
2008	2.2	0.2	1.5	0.2
2009	2.0	0.2	1.1	0.2
2010	2.0	0.2	1.2	0.2
2011	1.9	0.2	1.6	0.2

*Per 1,000 persons age 12 or older.
Source: Bureau of Justice Statistics, National Crime Victimization Survey, 1993–2011.

Numbers and rates for figure 5: Firearm homicides, by race, 1993–2010

	Number				Rate per 100,000 persons			
Year	White	Black	American Indian/ Alaska Native	Asian/Pacific Islander	White	Black	American Indian/ Alaska Native	Asian/Pacific Islander
1993	7,918	9,824	106	405	3.7	30.1	4.6	4.6
1994	7,774	9,302	123	328	3.6	28.0	5.2	3.6
1995	7,144	7,935	130	342	3.2	23.4	5.3	3.6
1996	6,240	7,403	90	304	2.8	21.5	3.6	3.0
1997	6,025	6,841	96	290	2.7	19.5	3.7	2.8
1998	5,412	6,053	99	234	2.4	17.0	3.6	2.2
1999	4,918	5,577	104	229	2.2	15.4	3.7	2.0
2000	4,806	5,699	86	210	2.1	15.6	2.9	1.8
2001	5,188	5,885	87	188	2.2	15.8	2.8	1.5
2002	5,185	6,285	117	242	2.2	16.7	3.7	1.9
2003	5,173	6,397	109	241	2.2	16.7	3.3	1.8
2004	5,119	6,201	104	200	2.2	16.0	3.0	1.4
2005	5,266	6,703	117	266	2.2	17.1	3.3	1.8
2006	5,279	7,113	119	280	2.2	17.9	3.2	1.9
2007	5,380	6,960	91	201	2.2	17.2	2.4	1.3
2008	5,305	6,569	97	208	2.2	16.0	2.4	1.3
2009	4,950	6,216	112	215	2.0	14.9	2.7	1.3
2010	4,647	6,151	113	167	1.9	14.6	2.7	1.0

Source: Centers for Disease Control and Prevention, National Center for Injury Prevention anc Control. Web-based Injury Statistics Query and Reporting System (WISQARS), 1993–2010. Retrieved March 2013 from www.cdc.gov/ncipc/wisqars.

Numbers and rates for figure 6: Firearm homicides, by Hispanic origin, 1993–2010

	Number		Rate per 100,000 persons	
Year	Hispanic	Non-Hispanic	Hispanic	Non-Hispanic
1993	3,192	14,597	12.4	6.3
1994	3,149	14,065	11.7	6.0
1995	3,008	12,260	10.7	5.2
1996	2,529	11,229	8.6	4.7
1997	2,298	10,868	7.4	4.5
1998	2,090	9,620	6.5	4.0
1999	1,939	8,821	5.7	3.6
2000	1,958	8,767	5.6	3.6
2001	2,123	9,134	5.7	3.7
2002	2,168	9,575	5.6	3.9
2003	2,316	9,536	5.8	3.8
2004	2,241	9,323	5.4	3.7
2005	2,453	9,835	5.7	3.9
2006	2,472	10,260	5.5	4.0
2007	2,385	10,193	5.2	4.0
2008	2,260	9,882	4.7	3.9
2009	2,115	9,275	4.3	3.6
2010	1,919	9,082	3.8	3.5

Source: Centers for Disease Control and Prevention, National Center for Injury Prevention and Control. Web-based Injury Statistics Query and Reporting System (WISQARS), 1993–2010. Retrieved March 2013 from www.cdc.gov/ncipc/wisqars.

APPENDIX TABLE 10
Rates and standard errors for figure 7: Nonfatal firearm violence, by race and Hispanic origin, 1994–2011

Year	White Rate*	White Standard error	Black Rate*	Black Standard error	Hispanic Rate*	Hispanic Standard error	American Indian/ Alaska Native Rate*	American Indian/ Alaska Native Standard error	Asian/Pacific Islander Rate*	Asian/Pacific Islander Standard error	Two or more races Rate*	Two or more races Standard error
1994	5.2	0.3	16.3	1.3	12.7	1.4	15.3 !	5.3	10.3	2.0	~	~
1995	4.6	0.3	14.2	1.1	12.1	1.1	16.3	4.9	4.9	1.1	~	~
1996	3.9	0.2	11.6	0.9	9.3	0.9	13.3 !	4.4	3.4	0.9	~	~
1997	4.0	0.3	9.4	0.9	6.9	0.8	3.7 !	2.6	2.0	0.7	~	~
1998	3.4	0.3	7.4	0.8	5.6	0.8	20.9 !	6.6	3.9	1.0	~	~
1999	2.2	0.2	7.9	0.9	5.0	0.8	25.1 !	7.5	4.0	1.1	~	~
2000	1.8	0.2	7.0	0.8	4.7	0.7	4.8 !	3.2	1.9	0.7	~	~
2001	2.0	0.2	5.0	0.7	3.8	0.6	1.1 !	1.5	1.5 !	0.6	~	~
2002	1.7	0.2	5.6	0.7	3.7	0.6	1.1 !	1.4	0.9 !	0.4	~	~
2003	1.5	0.2	5.7	0.7	2.6	0.4	--	~	1.0 !	0.5	~	~
2004	1.7	0.2	4.4	0.6	1.5	0.3	--	~	1.1 !	0.5	0.9 !	1.1
2005	1.6	0.2	4.2	0.7	2.2	0.4	--	~	1.2 !	0.5	2.8 !	2.0
2006	1.7	0.2	4.4	0.7	3.4	0.6	1.8 !	1.9	2.1 !	0.7	4.0 !	2.2
2007	1.4	0.2	7.1	0.9	3.0	0.5	3.3 !	2.4	1.7 !	0.6	4.7 !	2.1
2008	1.0	0.1	6.9	0.8	1.9	0.4	3.2 !	2.3	1.0 !	0.5	2.7 !	1.5
2009	0.9	0.1	5.1	0.7	1.7	0.4	2.9 !	2.3	0.9 !	0.4	1.4 !	1.2
2010	1.0	0.1	4.5	0.7	2.1	0.4	9.2 !	4.2	0.3 !	0.2	5.7 !	2.5
2011	1.4	0.1	2.8	0.4	2.2	0.4	8.6 !	3.4	0.6 !	0.3	7.6	2.3

*Per 1,000 persons age 12 or older.

! Interpret with caution. Estimate based on 10 or fewer sample cases, or coefficient of variation is greater than 50%.

~Not applicable.

--Less than 0.05.

Source: Bureau of Justice Statistics, National Crime Victimization Survey, 1993–2011.

APPENDIX TABLE 11
Numbers for table 4: Firearm homicides, by age, 1993–2011

Year	11 or younger	12–17	18–24	25–34	35–49	50 or older
1993	240	1,735	5,673	5,295	3,808	1,476
1994	176	1,736	5,435	5,059	3,700	1,399
1995	183	1,597	4,726	4,448	3,222	1,351
1996	178	1,295	4,334	3,918	3,030	1,266
1997	174	1,134	4,148	3,706	2,905	1,168
1998	157	888	3,753	3,231	2,669	1,082
1999	142	859	3,319	3,048	2,419	1,026
2000	110	709	3,371	3,074	2,488	1,037
2001	150	685	3,611	3,308	2,530	1,053
2002	151	721	3,708	3,465	2,646	1,125
2003	121	684	3,840	3,540	2,624	1,093
2004	105	763	3,485	3,503	2,533	1,214
2005	111	810	3,808	3,780	2,689	1,145
2006	142	940	4,030	3,767	2,688	1,216
2007	140	898	3,895	3,751	2,737	1,202
2008	140	844	3,662	3,612	2,655	1,264
2009	142	745	3,398	3,300	2,538	1,364
2010	127	708	3,273	3,331	2,294	1,340

Source: Centers for Disease Control and Prevention, National Center for Injury Prevention and Control. Web-based Injury Statistics Query and Reporting System (WISQARS), 1993–2010. Retrieved March 2013 from www.cdc.gov/ncipc/wisqars.

APPENDIX TABLE 12
Standard errors for table 4: Nonfatal firearm violence, by age, 1994–2011

Year	12-17	18-24	25-34	35-49	50 or older
1994	1.2	1.4	0.8	0.6	0.2
1995	0.9	1.2	0.6	0.4	0.2
1996	0.8	1.0	0.6	0.4	0.2
1997	0.8	1.1	0.6	0.4	0.2
1998	0.8	1.1	0.5	0.4	0.2
1999	0.7	1.0	0.6	0.3	0.2
2000	0.6	0.8	0.5	0.3	0.2
2001	0.5	0.8	0.4	0.3	0.2
2002	0.5	0.8	0.4	0.3	0.1
2003	0.5	0.7	0.4	0.2	0.1
2004	0.4	0.6	0.4	0.3	0.2
2005	0.4	0.7	0.5	0.3	0.2
2006	0.5	0.8	0.5	0.3	0.2
2007	0.7	0.7	0.5	0.3	0.2
2008	0.6	0.5	0.4	0.3	0.1
2009	0.3	0.6	0.4	0.3	0.1
2010	0.2	0.8	0.4	0.2	0.1
2011	0.3	0.6	0.3	0.2	0.1

*Rate per 1,000 persons age 12 or older.

!Interpret with caution. Estimate based on 10 or fewer sample cases, or coefficient of variation is greater than 50%.

Source: Bureau of Justice Statistics, National Crime Victimization Survey, 1993–2011.

APPENDIX TABLE 13
Numbers and rates for figure 8: Firearm homicides, by region, 1993–2011

Year	Number				Rate per 100,000 persons			
	Northeast	South	Midwest	West	Northeast	South	Midwest	West
1993	2,918	7,863	3,365	4,107	5.6	8.7	5.5	7.3
1994	2,489	7,577	3,391	4,070	4.8	8.3	5.5	7.1
1995	2,100	6,659	2,980	3,812	4.0	7.1	4.8	6.5
1996	1,838	6,248	2,791	3,160	3.5	6.6	4.4	5.3
1997	1,641	6,020	2,661	2,930	3.1	6.3	4.2	4.9
1998	1,347	5,434	2,490	2,527	2.5	5.6	3.9	4.1
1999	1,327	4,905	2,319	2,277	2.5	5.0	3.6	3.7
2000	1,391	4,846	2,284	2,280	2.6	4.8	3.6	3.6
2001	1,407	4,989	2,477	2,475	2.6	4.9	3.8	3.8
2002	1,406	5,292	2,381	2,750	2.6	5.1	3.7	4.2
2003	1,489	5,395	2,324	2,712	2.7	5.2	3.6	4.1
2004	1,485	5,164	2,212	2,763	2.7	4.9	3.4	4.1
2005	1,554	5,536	2,387	2,875	2.9	5.2	3.6	4.2
2006	1,715	5,701	2,505	2,870	3.2	5.2	3.8	4.2
2007	1,577	6,055	2,354	2,646	2.9	5.5	3.6	3.8
2008	1,506	5,778	2,439	2,456	2.7	5.2	3.7	3.5
2009	1,440	5,438	2,359	2,256	2.6	4.8	3.5	3.2
2010	1,552	5,082	2,296	2,148	2.8	4.4	3.4	3.0

Source:Centers for Disease Control and Prevention, National Center for Injury Prevention and Control. Web-based Injury Statistics Query and Reporting System (WISQARS), 1993–2010. Retrieved March 2013 from www.cdc.gov/ncipc/wisqars.

APPENDIX TABLE 14
Rates and standard errors for figure 9: Nonfatal firearm violence, by region, 1997–2011

Year	Northeast Rate*	Northeast Standard error	Midwest Rate*	Midwest Standard error	South Rate*	South Standard error	West Rate*	West Standard error
1997	3.1	0.4	4.7	0.5	5.4	0.4	5.7	0.5
1998	2.1	0.3	3.9	0.4	5.0	0.4	5.1	0.5
1999	1.4	0.3	3.0	0.4	3.6	0.4	4.9	0.5
2000	1.3	0.3	2.5	0.3	2.8	0.3	4.5	0.5
2001	1.4	0.3	2.6	0.4	3.0	0.3	2.8	0.4
2002	1.3	0.3	2.2	0.3	3.3	0.3	2.0	0.3
2003	1.0	0.2	2.1	0.3	2.9	0.3	1.9	0.3
2004	0.8	0.2	2.6	0.3	1.9	0.2	2.2	0.3
2005	0.9	0.2	2.8	0.4	1.9	0.3	1.9	0.3
2006	1.2	0.3	2.6	0.4	2.7	0.3	2.2	0.3
2007	0.9	0.2	2.1	0.3	3.5	0.4	1.9	0.3
2008	0.7	0.2	2.1	0.3	2.8	0.3	1.1	0.2
2009	0.8	0.2	2.0	0.3	1.7	0.2	1.4	0.3
2010	0.9	0.2	1.9	0.3	1.7	0.2	1.8	0.3
2011	1.3	0.2	1.7	0.3	1.9	0.2	1.8	0.3

*Rate per 1,000 persons age 12 or older.
Source: Bureau of Justice Statistics, National Crime Victimization Survey, 1996–2011.

APPENDIX TABLE 15
Rates and standard errors for figure 10: Nonfatal firearm violence, by urban-rural location, 1994–2011

Year	Urban Rate*	Urban Standard error	Suburban Rate*	Suburban Standard error	Rural Rate*	Rural Standard error
1994	10.6	0.7	6.3	0.4	5.2	0.5
1995	10.1	0.6	5.5	0.4	3.6	0.4
1996	8.4	0.5	4.4	0.3	3.1	0.4
1997	7.3	0.5	3.9	0.3	3.6	0.4
1998	6.2	0.5	3.8	0.3	2.3	0.3
1999	5.3	0.5	3.1	0.3	1.0	0.2
2000	4.8	0.5	2.3	0.2	1.0	0.2
2001	4.4	0.4	2.0	0.2	1.4	0.3
2002	4.4	0.4	1.8	0.2	1.1	0.2
2003	3.7	0.4	1.7	0.2	0.9	0.2
2004	3.0	0.3	1.7	0.2	1.0	0.2
2005	3.4	0.4	1.5	0.2	1.1	0.3
2006	3.3	0.4	1.8	0.2	1.9	0.4
2007	2.6	0.3	2.3	0.2	1.9	0.3
2008	2.2	0.3	1.8	0.2	1.2	0.3
2009	2.6	0.3	1.1	0.2	0.9	0.2
2010	2.8	0.3	1.2	0.2	0.7	0.2
2011	2.5	0.3	1.4	0.2	1.2	0.2

*Rate per 1,000 persons age 12 or older.
Source: Bureau of Justice Statistics, National Crime Victimization Survey, 1993–2011.

Rates and standard errors for table 5: Nonfatal firearm violence, by population size, 1997–2011

Year	Not a place Rate*	Not a place Standard error	Under 100,000 Rate*	Under 100,000 Standard error	100,000–249,999 Rate*	100,000–249,999 Standard error	250,000–499,999 Rate*	250,000–499,999 Standard error	500,000–999,999 Rate*	500,000–999,999 Standard error	1 million or more Rate*	1 million or more Standard error
1997	3.9	0.4	3.8	0.3	7.0	0.9	10.3	1.3	7.3	1.3	7.3	1.0
1998	3.0	0.3	3.9	0.3	4.8	0.8	7.0	1.1	9.2	1.6	5.7	0.9
1999	1.9	0.3	3.1	0.3	3.1	0.6	5.5	1.0	9.0	1.6	6.4	1.0
2000	1.5	0.2	2.2	0.2	3.9	0.7	6.5	1.1	6.3	1.3	5.6	0.9
2001	1.4	0.2	2.1	0.2	4.1	0.7	6.1	1.1	5.5	1.2	5.1	0.9
2002	1.2	0.2	2.3	0.2	2.8	0.6	3.9	0.8	4.9	1.1	5.3	0.8
2003	1.4	0.2	2.0	0.2	2.8	0.5	3.3	0.7	5.1	1.1	3.6	0.7
2004	1.4	0.2	1.4	0.2	3.0	0.6	4.1	0.9	5.5	1.2	2.7	0.6
2005	1.2	0.2	1.6	0.2	2.9	0.6	3.6	0.9	4.5	1.2	4.6	0.9
2006	1.6	0.2	2.1	0.2	2.6	0.6	2.6	0.8	3.8	1.0	4.9	0.9
2007	1.5	0.2	2.6	0.3	2.7	0.5	2.4	0.7	5.4	1.1	2.1	0.5
2008	0.8	0.2	2.1	0.2	2.1	0.5	3.2	0.8	4.9	1.0	1.4	0.4
2009	0.9	0.2	1.1	0.2	2.2	0.5	3.0	0.8	4.0	1.0	3.5	0.7
2010	0.9	0.2	1.2	0.2	1.8	0.5	2.8	0.8	5.1	1.1	4.0	0.8
2011	1.4	0.2	1.2	0.2	1.3	0.3	3.9	0.8	4.6	0.9	3.2	0.6

*Rate per 1,000 persons age 12 or older.

Source: Bureau of Justice Statistics, National Crime Victimization Survey, 1996–2011.

Standard errors for table 6: Nonfatal firearm and nonfirearm violence, by victim-offender relationship, 2007–2011

Relationship to victim	Total nonfatal violence	Firearm violence Number	Firearm violence Percent of total violence	Nonfirearm violence Number	Nonfirearm violence Percent of total violence
Total	520,018	107,331	0.3%	495,683	0.4%
Nonstranger	351,653	56,980	0.3	341,349	0.4
Intimate	167,301	27,453	0.6	163,040	0.6
Other relative	105,593	24,480	1.1	100,985	.2
Friend/acquaintance	247,394	39,620	0.4	240,775	0.5
Stranger	281,855	74,319	0.6	262,843	0.7
Unknown	126,046	34,768	1.1	118,113	.2

Source: Bureau of Justice Statistics, National Crime Victimization Survey, 2007–2011.

Standard errors for table 7: Nonfatal firearm and nonfirearm violence, by location of crime, 2007–2011

Location	Total nonfatal violence		Firearm violence		Nonfirearm violence	
	Number	Percent	Total number	Percent	Total number	Percent
Total	520,094	~	107,331	~	495,761	~
Victims home or lodging	204,185	0.6%	42,032	1.6%	195,889	0.6%
Near victim's home	170,118	0.5	46,062	1.8	159,113	0.5
In, at, or near a friend, neighbor, or relative's home	106,117	0.3	22,283	1.0	102,275	0.3
Commercial place	125,178	0.4	27,429	1.2	120,070	0.4
Parking lot or garage	91,497	0.3	37,086	1.5	80,309	0.3
School	150,761	0.5	6,544	0.3	150,471	0.5
Open area, on street, or public transportation	166,506	0.5	46,260	1.8	155,261	0.5
Other location	128,572	0.4	18,853	0.8	126,101	0.4

~Not applicable.

Source: Bureau of Justice Statistics, National Crime Victimization Survey, 2007–2011.

Standard errors for table 9: Nonfatal firearm and nonfirearm violence, by injury and treatment received, 2007–2011

Injury and treatment	Total nonfatal violence		Firearm violence		Nonfirearm violence	
	Number	Percent	Total number	Percent	Total number	Percent
Injury	520,094	~	107,331	~	495,761	~
Not injured	435,239	0.7%	92,106	1.8%	414,216	0.7%
Injured	221,742	0.6	46,376	1.8	212,304	0.6
Serious injuries	76,874	0.2	23,654	1.0	73,196	0.3
Gun shot	12,758	--	12,758	0.6	~	~
Minor injuries	189,519	0.5	38,061	1.5	182,281	0.6
Rape without other injuries	39,058	0.1	4,232	0.2	38,750	0.1
Treatment for injury	221,742	~	46,376	~	212,304	~
No treatment	159,205	1.3%	22,999	3.7%	156,054	1.3%
Any treatment	130,902	1.2	38,813	3.8	121,399	1.3
Treatment setting	130,902	~	38,813	~	121,399	~
At the scene/home of victim, neighbor, or friend/ other location	70,643	1.7%	15,653	3.8%	68,065	1.9%
In doctor's office, hospital emergency room, or overnight at hospital	101,753	1.8	34,730	3.8	92,599	1.9

--Less than 0.05%.

~Not applicable.

Source: Bureau of Justice Statistics, National Crime Victimization Survey, 2007–2011.

Numbers and standard errors for figure 11: Nonfatal firearm injuries, 2001–2011

Year	Number	Standard error
2001	41,044	10,287
2002	37,321	9,282
2003	42,505	11,558
2004	43,592	11,764
2005	50,320	14,431
2006	52,748	15,027
2007	48,676 !	15,139
2008	56,626	16,648
2009	44,466	11,767
2010	53,738	15,769
2011	55,544	15,671

! Interpret with caution. Estimate based on fewer than 20 NEISS cases (based on unweighted data), national estimates less than 1,200 (based on weighted data), or the coefficient of variation (CV) of the estimate greater than 30%.

Source: Consumer Product Safety Commission, National Electronic Injury Surveillance System All Injury Program (NEISS-AIP), 2001–2011, accessed from the National Center for Injury Prevention and Control, CDC.

Standard errors for table 10: Nonfatal firearm and nonfirearm violence reported and not reported to police, 2007–2011

	Total nonfatal violence	Firearm violence	Nonfirearm violence
Total	~	~	~
Reported	0.7%	2.1%	0.7%
Not reported	0.7	2.1	0.8
Reason not reported	~	~	~
Dealt with it another way	0.9%	2.1%	0.9%
Not important enough to respondent	0.7	1.6	0.7
Police could not or would not do anything to help	0.7	3.0	0.7
Fear of reprisal	0.4	3.1	0.4
Did not want to get offender in trouble with law, or advised not to report	0.4	1.3	0.4
Other, unknown, or not one most important reason	0.7	2.6	0.7

~Not applicable.

Source: Bureau of Justice Statistics, National Crime Victimization Survey, 2007–2011.

Standard errors for table 11: Self-protective behaviors, by type of crime, 2007–2011

Self-protective behavior	Violent crime		Property crime	
	Total number	Percent	Total number	Percent
Total	520,094	~	619,179	~
Offered no resistance	312,558	0.7%	295,645	0.3%
Threatened or attacked with a firearm	30,347	0.1	24,437	--
Threatened or attacked with other weapon	40,012	0.1	14,630	--
Threatened or attacked without a weapon	205,362	0.6	51,411	0.1
Nonconfrontational tactics	227,856	0.6	90,178	0.1
Other reaction	90,004	0.3	36,683	--
Unknown reaction	12,068	--	8,176	--
Victim was not present	~	~	641,196	0.4

~Not applicable.

--Less than 0.05%.

Source: Bureau of Justice Statistics, National Crime Victimization Survey, 2007–2011.

www.ingramcontent.com/pod-product-compliance
Lightning Source LLC
Chambersburg PA
CBHW081811280526
45789CB00008B/3096